CHUCK SCHUMER

By Therese Shea

BOTH SIDES of the Aisle

Enslow PUBLISHING

Please visit our website, www.enslow.com. For a free color catalog of all our high-quality books, call toll free 1-800-398-2504 or fax 1-877-980-4454.

Cataloging-in-Publication Data

Names: Shea, Therese.
Title: Chuck Schumer / Therese Shea.
Description: Buffalo, NY : Enslow Publishing, 2026. | Series: Both sides of the aisle | Includes glossary and index.
Identifiers: ISBN 9781978546561 (pbk.) | ISBN 9781978546578 (library bound) | ISBN 9781978546585 (ebook)
Subjects: LCSH: United States. Congress. Senate–Biography–Juvenile literature. | United States. Congress. House–Biography–Juvenile literature. | United States. Congress. Senate–Juvenile literature. | Legislators–United States–Biography–Juvenile literature. | Schumer, Charles E.
Classification: LCC E840.8 S54 2026 | DDC 328.73092–dc23

Published in 2026 by
Enslow Publishing
2544 Clinton Street
Buffalo, NY 14224

Designer: Andrea Davison-Bartolotta
Editor: Therese Shea

Photo credits: Cover (main), p. 1 lev radin/Shutterstock.com; cover, p. 1 (buildings) Fandorina Liza/Shutterstock.com; series art (background stars) v_kulieva/Shutterstock.com; series art (watercolor background) Apostrophe/Shutterstock.com; p. 5 File:Chuck Schumer official photo.jpg/Wikimedia Commons; p. 7 Leonard Zhukovsky/Shutterstock.com; p. 8 File:Schumer-1987-.jpg/Wikimedia Commons; p. 9 Framalicious/Shutterstock.com; pp. 11, 15 Ron Adar/Shutterstock.com; p. 12 File:111th US Senate class photo.jpg/Wikimedia Commons; p. 13 Stuart Monk/Shutterstock.com; p. 17 File:Chuck Schumer meets with Ketanji Brown Jackson.jpg/Wikimedia Commons; p. 19 Anderson Photo/Shutterstock.com.

Printed in the United States of America

CPSIA compliance information: Batch #CWENS26: For further information contact Enslow Publishing, at 1-800-398-2504.

CONTENTS

Words in the glossary appear in **bold** type the first time they are used in the text.

MEET CHUCK

Chuck Schumer is New York's longest serving U.S. senator ever. He's the leader of the Democrats in the Senate and often speaks for the entire Democratic political party in Congress. Because of that, Schumer is often in the news.

Schumer has worked in public service through the government for nearly his whole adult life. Because of this, he has a deep knowledge of how state and federal, or national, government works. His life in **politics** began in New York City.

MORE TO **KNOW**

Schumer is a member of the Democratic Party. A political party is a group of people with similar beliefs about how a government should be run.

Chuck Schumer is the senior U.S. senator of New York. This means he has served longer than New York's other senator, Kirsten Gillibrand.

A NEW YORKER

Charles "Chuck" Ellis Schumer was born November 23, 1950, in Brooklyn, in New York City. He was the oldest of Abe and Selma Schumer's three children. Chuck was a gifted student. He had a perfect score on the SAT, a pre-college test. He was also the valedictorian, or top of his class, at James Madison High School.

In 1967, Schumer began at Harvard College where he studied science at first. However, he became interested in politics after working for Eugene McCarthy's **campaign** for president in 1968.

MORE TO KNOW

Abe Schumer ran a pest control business. When Chuck was elected to government office, he remembered Abe's many challenges as a small business owner.

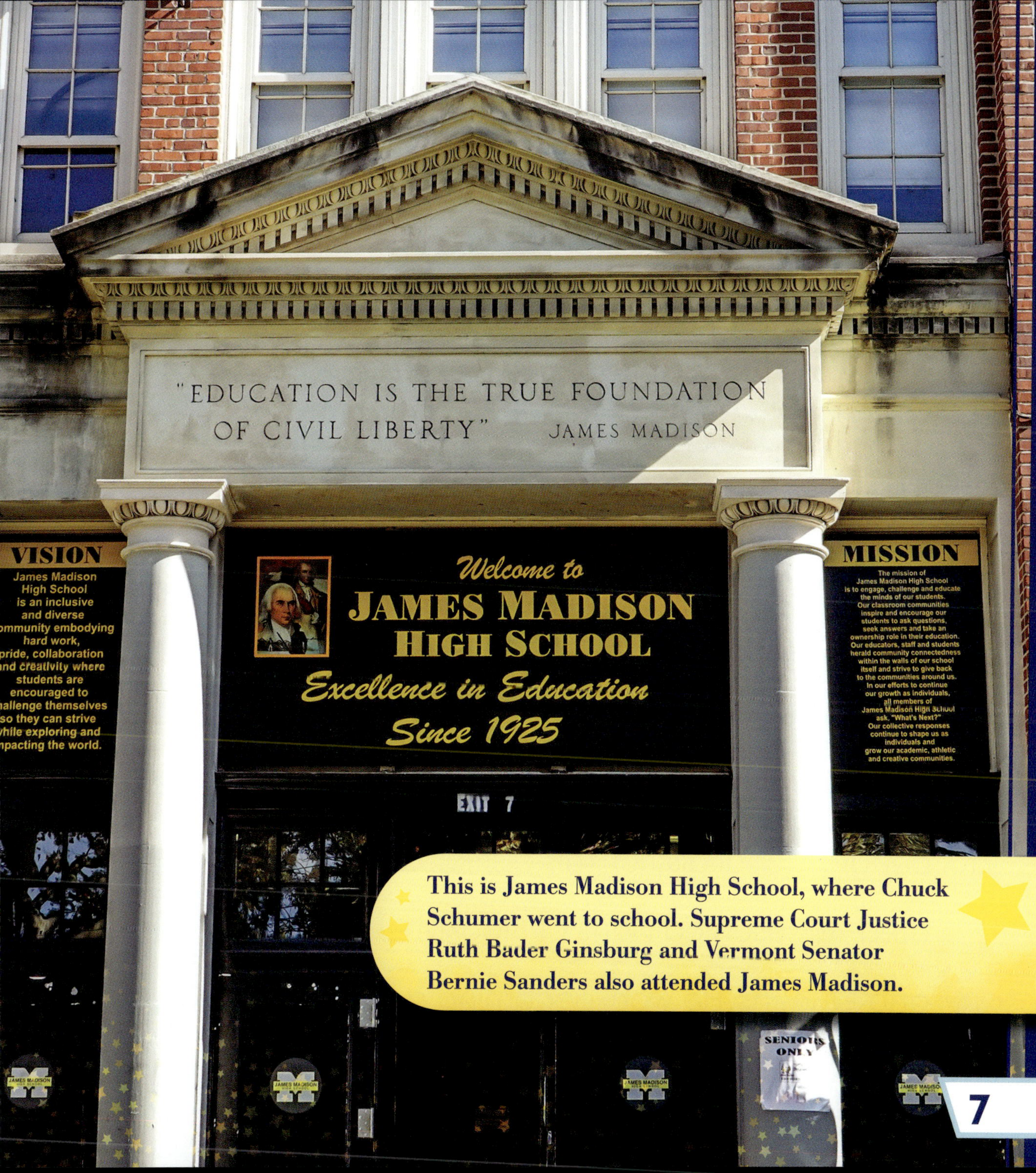

This is James Madison High School, where Chuck Schumer went to school. Supreme Court Justice Ruth Bader Ginsburg and Vermont Senator Bernie Sanders also attended James Madison.

FROM LAW SCHOOL TO POLITICS

After college, Schumer went on to Harvard Law School. When he finished in 1974, he decided not to become a lawyer. Instead, he went into state politics. He ran for a seat in the New York State Assembly in 1974 and won. He served three terms in the assembly, from 1975 to 1981.

In 1980, Schumer decided to run for a seat in the U.S. House of Representatives, for New York's 16th congressional district. This district, or area, represented parts of Brooklyn and Queens. He won, becoming a U.S. representative in January 1981.

MORE TO KNOW

Like Congress, the New York State Legislature, or lawmaking body, is made up of two parts: the New York State Senate and the New York State Assembly.

U.S. Congress is the lawmaking part of the federal government. It's made up of the House of Representatives and the Senate. Both meet in the Capitol, shown here.

WORKING IN THE HOUSE

Schumer served in the U.S. House of Representatives from 1981 to 1999. During that time, he worked on laws to fight crime. He was a **sponsor** of the **Violence** Against Women Act, which aimed to keep women safer from certain kinds of crimes. He also sponsored the Brady **Bill**, which would become a gun control law.

In addition, Schumer worked on laws that made banks and credit cards tell users about fees in an easy-to-understand way. Surprise fees were costing people a lot of money.

MORE TO **KNOW**

U.S. representatives serve two-year terms, while U.S. senators serve six-year terms.

As a New York congressman, Chuck Schumer spends time in both Washington, DC, and in New York.

ON TO THE SENATE

After 18 years as a U.S. representative, Schumer decided to run for Senate in 1998. He defeated, or beat, Republican Al D'Amato, who had held the seat for three terms. As a U.S. senator, Schumer now represented the entire state of New York.

One of his focuses was his state's **economy**. He asked companies to come to New York to create new jobs for New Yorkers. He worked on a law to make colleges easier to pay for. He also supported programs to help New York farmers.

U.S. SENATE CHAMBER

One senator alone can't make a bill become a law. Senators have to work with other lawmakers to gather support. They need a certain number of members of Congress to vote for the bill.

MORE TO KNOW

Schumer married Iris Weinshall in 1980. They have two daughters, Jessica and Alison.

SENATE LEADER

Beginning in 2017, Schumer was elected by other Democratic senators to be Senate minority leader. The minority leader is the spokesperson for the political party that is the minority, or smaller number, in the Senate.

Schumer became the Senate majority leader from 2021 to 2025. At that time, there were more Democrats than Republicans in the Senate. Majority and minority leaders make key decisions, such as which senators can be on different committees. Committees are groups that focus on certain issues, such as the federal **budget**, health, and the **environment**.

MORE TO KNOW

Schumer was the first New Yorker to serve as Senate majority leader.

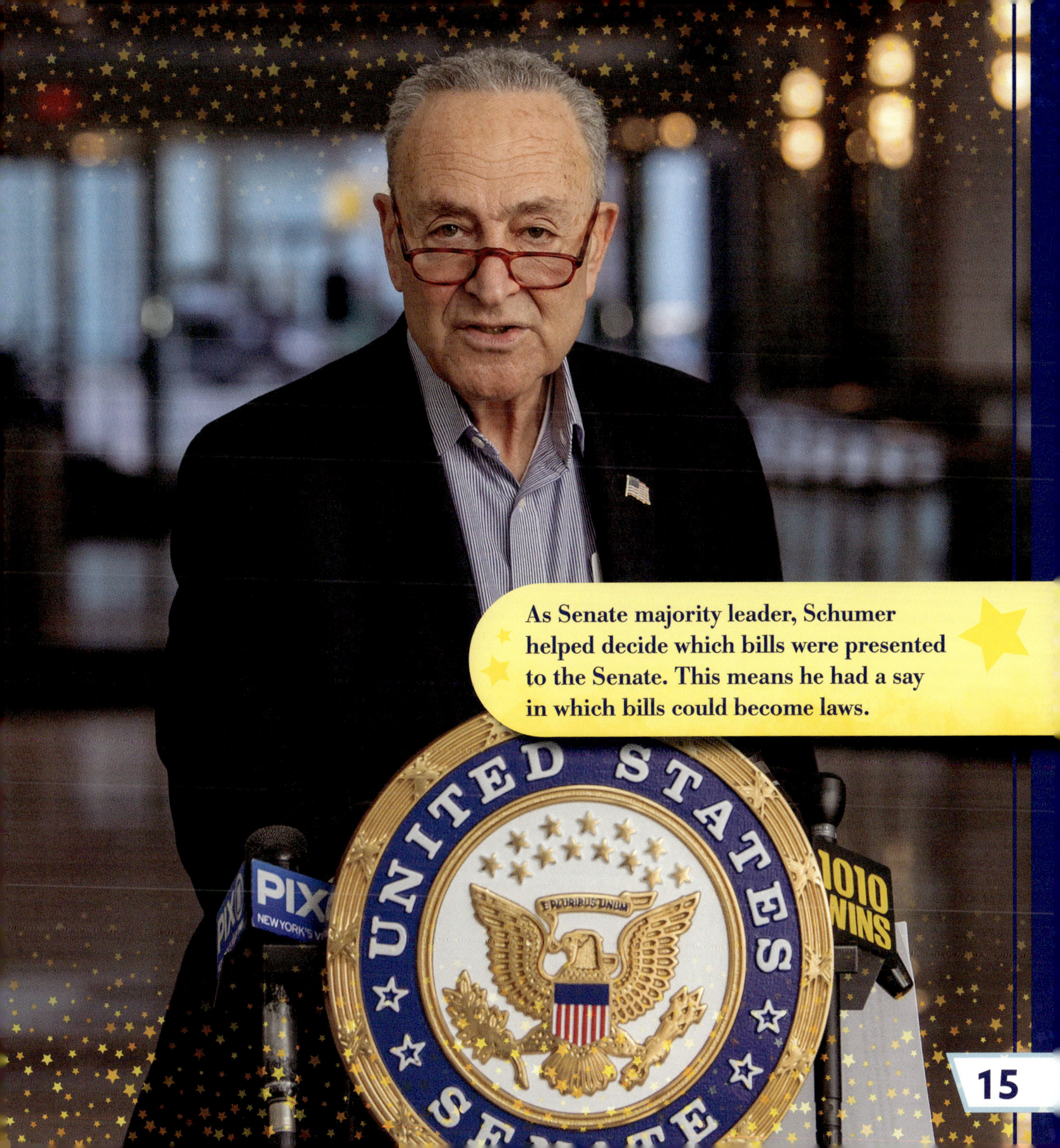

As Senate majority leader, Schumer helped decide which bills were presented to the Senate. This means he had a say in which bills could become laws.

AID AND IMPROVEMENTS

As Senate majority leader, Schumer supported certain bills over others. In 2021, the American Rescue Plan Act provided aid to people during the COVID-19 **pandemic**. That same year, the **Infrastructure** Investment and Jobs Act was passed to fix and improve U.S. infrastructure, such as roads, bridges, railways, power grids, and internet access.

In 2022, the CHIPS and Science Act was passed to boost science and **technology** projects in the nation. Schumer was proud of these federal laws. In 2022, he was elected to a record fifth term to the Senate.

As Senate majority leader in 2022, Schumer also played a role in the confirmation, or official approving, of Ketanji Brown Jackson (shown here) to the U.S. Supreme Court.

MORE TO KNOW

The Infrastructure Investment and Jobs Act was also known as the Bipartisan Infrastructure Law. "Bipartisan" is a word that means both political parties supported it.

CALLS FOR COMPROMISE

In 2024, Republicans won the majority in the Senate. Schumer took the role of Senate minority leader again. The Democrats and Republicans are often at odds. Sometimes compromises must happen. A compromise is a way of two sides reaching an agreement in which each gives up something.

Compromise isn't easy between political parties. Members of Congress have different needs and wants for their states and different ideas about what's best for the country. Schumer has said, "Our responsibility is clear: we need to put the needs of our country above the interests of party politics."

Schumer and other members of Congress decide when to compromise and when to refuse to compromise.

MORE TO KNOW

In 2025, Schumer voted for a Republican bill to **fund** the government. Many Democrats were unhappy with this compromise. Schumer believed his choice avoided a worse outcome.

SCHUMER ON THE MOVE

As one of the most famous people in Congress, Schumer is often in the news. In fact, other members of Congress joke about that. But he uses his spotlight to bring attention to issues he cares about. These could be issues in small New York towns or those affecting the entire nation.

When Schumer wants to think, he steps away from the camera and hops on his bike. He sometimes stops to chat with people. He asks questions and listens to answers. This long-time congressman wants to be a local and national leader.

CHUCK SCHUMER TIMELINE

1950	Charles "Chuck" Ellis Schumer is born November 23 in Brooklyn, New York.
1967	He is the valedictorian of his class at James Madison High School.
1968	While at Harvard, he becomes interested in politics through working on Eugene McCarthy's presidential campaign.
1974	He graduates from Harvard Law School and wins a seat in the New York Assembly.
1980	He wins the NY-16 seat in the U.S. House of Representatives.
1998	He wins a seat in the U.S. Senate.
2017	He is elected to be Senate minority leader.
2021	Schumer is the first New Yorker elected to be Senate majority leader.
2022	He is elected to a record fifth term in the Senate.
2025	He becomes the Senate minority leader again.

Schumer hopes to be a leader who can unify, or bring together, the Democratic Party to address the needs of the nation.

GLOSSARY

bill: An idea for a law that has been introduced to Congress.

budget: A plan for collecting money and spending money over a period of time.

campaign: A planned group of activities to achieve an aim, such as winning an election.

economy: The money made in an area and how it is made.

environment: The natural world in which a plant or animal lives.

fund: To provide money for a group or activity.

infrastructure: The basic physical structures, such as roads and transportation systems, needed by an organization, region, or country.

pandemic: A time when a disease, or sickness, spreads quickly and affects a large number of people in a place or throughout the world.

politics: The activities of the government and government officials.

sponsor: A lawmaker who presents a bill to a legislature. Those who support it may be called cosponsors.

technology: Using science, engineering, and other industries to invent useful tools or to solve problems. Also a machine, piece of equipment, or method created by technology.

violence: The use of force to harm someone.

FOR MORE INFORMATION

Books

Anderson, Ted. *History Tipsters Climb Capitol Hill: The Inside Scoop on U.S. Congress*. North Mankato, MN: Capstone Press, 2025.

Stratton, Connor. *Congress*. Lake Elmo, MN: Focus Readers, 2024.

Websites

Chuck Schumer Facts for Kids
kids.kiddle.co/Chuck_Schumer
Read more about Schumer's early life and career.

Senator Chuck Schumer
www.schumer.senate.gov
The official Senate website for Chuck Schumer has many facts about his work in Congress.

INDEX